a gift to

_____

from

_____

THE
heart
OF A
DOG

writings from Liz Abeler Blaylock

KPT PUBLISHING

ABOUT THE AUTHOR

LIZ ABELER BLAYLOCK lives in Minnesota with her husband and a cat. She called on her brother and his family—dog lovers—to bring about this story: life with a dog.

By day, Liz works with middle school special-needs students. By night, she makes dinner, does laundry, moving piles of stuff from one place to another, and makes time for her cat.

"I marvel at the intricate,
beautiful, and fearful working of creation,
and revel in the grace and mercy of the Creator."

Enjoy my memories!

I promise
to *always* love
the hand
that feeds me.

I do this
trusting you
will share.

Heaven!

Without us,
your heart
would be
empty.

Could you *even* imagine life without me?

Couldn't stop
with just one,
could you?

I'm simple.

Add cookies...
and the love will
just *ooze* out.

Brown and black.
White and brown.

Same loyalty inside.

What do you
mean *my bark*?

Have you seen my
ferocious tail?

If I *need* this hat,
should we even
be outside?

Admit it.

My eyes are *irresistible*.

"No."
"No."
"No."

Could you say
just one
encouraging word.

Why would someone bury a perfectly good flip-flop?

So, what *will* I do on vacation?

Am I white
with
black spots…

or black
with
white spots?

Darling as we may be…
we can still *clear* a room
in less than a minute!

"What-to-
pee-on"
intensive
training.

How was I
supposed to know
what it was
until I rolled in it?

Can I keep them?

What I
really need
is a good scratch
behind the ears.

SQUIRREL!

A good fence
is you and me
on the *same* side.

Is he home *yet*?

I may be *old*,
but how 'bout
a few tosses
with that *new* stick?

"Okay" to the bow,
but not
the nail polish.

NEW RULE FOR
DOG–OWNER'S MANUAL:

Hug. *Daily*.

The Heart of a Dog

© 2018 KPT Publishing, LLC
Written by Liz Abeler Blaylock

Published by KPT Publishing
Minneapolis, Minnesota 55406
www.KPTPublishing.com

ISBN 978-1-944833-48-0

Designed by AbelerDesign.com

First printing November 2018

10 9 8 7 6 5 4 3 2

Printed in the United States of America